AI Social Media Ads Manager

Automate Campaigns Across All Platforms

By Joe Correa

Published by Live Stronger Faster

This book is for educational and informational purposes only. The author and publisher are not engaged in rendering legal, financial, or other professional advice. Readers should consult a qualified professional before making any financial decisions.

First Edition

Table of Contents

Introduction to AI Social Media Ads Manager

In today's hyper-connected world, managing social media advertising has evolved far beyond simply posting an image or running a single campaign. The average business now runs simultaneous campaigns on Facebook, Instagram, YouTube, TikTok, LinkedIn, and X (formerly Twitter). Each platform demands different ad formats, creative strategies, audience targeting methods, and metrics of success. Trying to keep up manually is not just exhausting—it's nearly impossible. That's why artificial intelligence is completely transforming how ads are created, scheduled, tested, and optimized. With the help of AI social media ads management tools, what once took an entire marketing department can now be handled by a single person with a smart dashboard and automated workflows.

This book, *AI Social Media Ads Manager: Automate Campaigns Across All Platforms*, is your complete guide to mastering multi-platform automation. Whether you're a small business owner, a digital marketer, or an agency professional, you'll learn how to centralize your entire ad strategy under one intelligent system powered by AI. Imagine a world where you no longer have to log into multiple platforms to adjust budgets, monitor conversions, or analyze performance.

Instead, your AI ads manager pulls data from every network—Meta, TikTok, Google, YouTube, and more—and gives you actionable insights, automatic optimization suggestions, and predictive analytics that tell you exactly where your next dollar should go.

AI-powered advertising is about more than efficiency—it's about strategy. Machine learning algorithms can detect patterns invisible to humans. They can recognize the best-performing ad creatives, identify audience segments that are likely to convert, and forecast campaign outcomes based on past behavior. This gives marketers the ability to predict trends before they happen. With AI scheduling and automation tools, you can plan months of content and advertising across multiple networks while maintaining consistency in voice, branding, and message. You can automatically adjust campaigns based on real-time data, pausing underperforming ads and reallocating budgets to high-performing ones—all without lifting a finger.

One of the greatest challenges in modern digital marketing is fragmentation. You may have an ad that performs well on Facebook but falls flat on TikTok. Your YouTube video might generate engagement but not leads. AI solves this by unifying your campaigns under one analytics-driven strategy. Using AI cross-platform marketing tools, you can now see how each network contributes to your overall funnel—from first impression to final conversion. These systems generate unified analytics reports that give you a complete overview of performance and ROI, allowing you to make smarter business decisions instantly.

Another breakthrough in this space is natural language processing (NLP), the same technology that powers ChatGPT and other AI marketing tools. These systems understand the nuances of tone, audience intent, and contextual meaning across platforms. For example, AI can automatically rewrite a Facebook caption into a more concise TikTok hook or expand a YouTube ad description into an SEO-rich version for Google Display. This means you can maintain platform-specific optimization while ensuring your message remains unified and brand-consistent everywhere.

AI ad management platforms like Sprinklr, Hootsuite AI, AdCreative.ai, and HubSpot's Marketing Hub are already changing the landscape of multi-platform campaigns. They integrate directly with Meta Ads Manager, Google Ads, TikTok Ads, and LinkedIn Campaign Manager to streamline your workflow. These tools allow automated A/B testing, intelligent scheduling, and predictive analytics that reduce human error and increase campaign profitability. Instead of reacting to results after they happen, you'll use AI to act before your competition even knows what's coming. Throughout this book, you'll explore how to set up a truly automated system—from connecting your ad accounts to using AI analytics for reporting and performance optimization. You'll discover how to use AI scheduling tools to maintain a consistent posting rhythm, how to generate unified reports that reveal what's really driving your conversions, and how to use predictive modeling to plan future campaigns. You'll also learn about advanced AI tools for data visualization, creative automation, and audience management, giving you a 360-degree view of your digital ecosystem.

As we move deeper into the age of automation, marketing success will depend less on who works the hardest and more on who automates the smartest. AI marketing tools don't replace creativity—they amplify it. They give marketers the freedom to focus on what truly matters: crafting powerful messages and building emotional connections with audiences. With an AI-driven system managing your campaigns, you'll spend less time inside dashboards and more time innovating, scaling, and growing your brand.

This book will not only show you how to use AI tools—it will help you think like an AI strategist. You'll understand how to train your systems, interpret data intelligently, and create adaptive marketing ecosystems that learn, evolve, and self-correct. Each chapter builds on the last, walking you step-by-step through setup, automation, optimization, and long-term scaling strategies. By the end, you'll have the knowledge to create campaigns that practically run themselves—and the confidence to manage millions in ad spend with precision and ease.

Welcome to the future of advertising—where data meets creativity, automation meets intelligence, and marketing meets limitless potential. The AI revolution in social media advertising is here, and with this book, you'll be at the forefront of it. Get ready to transform your digital marketing into an automated powerhouse that works 24/7, drives consistent growth, and positions your brand ahead of every curve in the fast-moving world of AI-powered marketing.

Chapter 1: The Evolution of Social Media Advertising

Social media advertising has undergone a dramatic transformation in the last decade. What began as a simple tool for increasing visibility on platforms like Facebook has evolved into a multi-channel, data-driven ecosystem fueled by artificial intelligence. In the early 2010s, marketers were excited just to have the ability to target users by age, location, and interests. Campaigns were mostly static—images, headlines, and short blurbs tested manually, often relying on guesswork and time-consuming split tests. Fast-forward to today, and every major advertising platform is integrated with machine learning, automation, and real-time analytics. The entire marketing landscape now revolves around one question: how can we let AI handle the complexity while we focus on creativity and strategy?

AI social media advertising represents the next phase of digital evolution. Instead of reacting to campaign results days or weeks after launch, AI systems analyze millions of data points instantly, predicting which ad creative, headline, or video is most likely to convert. This shift eliminates much of the guesswork that once defined social media marketing. What's more, the introduction of AI-powered tools allows even solo entrepreneurs to compete with enterprise-level marketing teams. A single person can now manage campaigns across multiple platforms—Facebook, Instagram, TikTok, YouTube, and LinkedIn—with precision once only possible for corporations with massive budgets.

At the heart of this revolution is automation. AI automates campaign creation, targeting, and optimization by using algorithms that continuously learn from user behavior. These systems observe who interacts with your content, what they click, how long they watch a video, and which actions they take next. Then, they automatically adjust targeting, budget allocation, and ad placements based on what's working. The result is not just efficiency—it's exponential improvement. Campaigns that once plateaued after a few weeks now evolve dynamically, optimizing themselves without your constant intervention.

Cross-platform integration is another major breakthrough. Traditionally, advertisers had to log into multiple dashboards—Meta Ads Manager, Google Ads, TikTok Business Center, and LinkedIn Campaign Manager—to track performance. Now, AI ads managers consolidate all of that into a single unified dashboard. This means one login, one control center, and one data-driven strategy across every major platform. You can view your cost-per-lead across

Facebook and YouTube simultaneously, compare ad creatives from TikTok to Instagram, and instantly identify which platform delivers the highest ROI. This holistic view gives you an unprecedented advantage in resource allocation and campaign scalability.

Predictive analytics is the brain of the AI advertising ecosystem. Instead of waiting to see what works, AI uses historical data and behavioral patterns to predict outcomes. For example, if your past campaigns showed that 25-to-35-year-old entrepreneurs in urban areas tend to click on 6-second TikTok clips featuring upbeat music and short captions, your AI system will prioritize creating and testing similar ad variations. Over time, it learns your brand voice, creative preferences, and audience behavior so that each campaign becomes smarter than the last. You're not just running ads—you're training a digital intelligence to market for you.

But with great automation comes the need for great oversight. Successful marketers must balance data-driven automation with human intuition. AI can recommend when to post, who to target, and which creative performs best, but it's the marketer's job to ensure the message remains authentic and emotionally resonant. This partnership between human creativity and artificial intelligence is the foundation of the next era of advertising. When used correctly, AI doesn't replace marketers—it multiplies their impact. It gives creative professionals the freedom to focus on storytelling, brand building, and innovation rather than repetitive technical tasks.

The businesses that thrive in this new era are those that embrace agility. The pace of technological change in social media advertising is relentless. Platforms like Meta, Google, and TikTok roll out AI features every month—from automated creative testing to AI-generated headlines and captions. Marketers who adopt these tools early gain a massive competitive advantage. They can launch faster, test more variations, and scale successful campaigns before others even realize what's happening. Mastering AI social media ads management is not just about learning a new toolset—it's about adopting a new mindset of constant innovation and smart automation.

This first chapter is about understanding the shift that brought us here. The tools, technologies, and strategies that once defined marketing are becoming obsolete. Manual optimization, isolated analytics, and single-platform strategies no longer suffice. The future belongs to marketers who think like data scientists but act like storytellers—those who can harness artificial intelligence to enhance human creativity. As you progress through this book, you'll learn how to implement this philosophy practically—how to connect your accounts, automate scheduling, unify analytics, and scale campaigns seamlessly across every major platform. But first, it's essential to grasp the core truth: AI is not the future of advertising—it is the present. And those who learn to master it now will lead the industry for years to come.

One System That Could Do The Work

It was 2:00 a.m. when Maria leaned back in her chair, staring at six open tabs on her laptop—Facebook Ads Manager, Google Ads, TikTok Business Center, Instagram Insights, YouTube Analytics, and a spreadsheet filled with color-coded numbers. She was exhausted. As the founder of a small digital marketing agency, she managed campaigns for seven clients, each on multiple platforms. Her phone buzzed constantly with notifications about ad spend limits, underperforming creatives, and missed optimization windows. Maria loved marketing, but the endless manual updates and analysis had turned her passion into chaos.

Then, one day, everything changed. While scrolling through LinkedIn, she stumbled upon an article titled *"The Rise of AI-Powered Social Media Ad Managers."* Curious, she clicked—and what she read felt like a glimpse into the future she had been waiting for. The article described how new AI dashboards could connect to all her ad platforms, automate scheduling, and even analyze which creatives were performing best across different audiences. The idea sounded almost too good to be true: one system that could do the work of an entire team.

The next morning, Maria signed up for a trial of one of the top-rated AI ad management platforms. Within minutes, she connected all her clients' accounts and watched as the system began analyzing her campaigns in real time. By noon, the AI had flagged underperforming Facebook ads and suggested better-performing variations from her TikTok campaigns. It automatically paused ads that were wasting money and reallocated that budget toward the videos with the highest engagement. Maria had done nothing—yet her return on ad spend increased by 22% in a single day.

Over the next few weeks, Maria experienced something she hadn't felt in years: creative freedom. Instead of spending hours every morning managing dashboards, she started brainstorming new campaign ideas, testing bold video concepts, and refining her brand storytelling. The AI handled the data while she focused on the art. It was like having a team of analysts working around the clock—except they never slept, never made mistakes, and constantly got smarter.

Her clients noticed the difference almost immediately. “Whatever you’re doing,” one of them said on a Zoom call, “keep doing it. Our leads have doubled.” Maria smiled, knowing that her secret weapon wasn’t just more effort—it was automation. The AI had learned which demographics were converting, which videos performed best during certain hours, and which platforms produced the highest lifetime value customers. It was as if the system had developed a sixth sense for marketing intuition.

A few months later, Maria’s small agency transformed into a powerhouse. She hired her first two assistants—not to manage ads, but to create more content. The AI system had freed up 80% of her time, and her revenue had tripled. She even began consulting other agencies, teaching them how to implement AI-driven ad strategies. What once seemed like an impossible workload had become a fully automated ecosystem running almost on autopilot. The story of Maria’s agency became a testament to a new era in marketing—one where human creativity and artificial intelligence worked hand in hand to achieve extraordinary results.

As her business continued to grow, Maria realized that the AI wasn’t just optimizing campaigns—it was optimizing her life. She finally had time to spend with her family, travel, and explore new ideas. Her clients thrived, her brand grew, and her confidence soared. What started as a desperate search for efficiency turned into a complete transformation of how she worked, thought, and lived.

The lesson was clear: automation wasn't about replacing people—it was about liberating them. By trusting AI to manage the repetitive, data-heavy side of marketing, Maria unlocked her full creative potential. The same opportunity exists for every marketer willing to embrace change. The question is no longer whether AI can manage your campaigns—the question is whether you're ready to let it.

Chapter 2: Setting Up Your AI Social Media Ad System

The first step to building a truly automated advertising machine is setting up your AI social media ad system. This is where structure meets intelligence — where the foundation of every future campaign begins. Before automation, creativity, and analytics can work together, you need a reliable and organized system that connects all your social media accounts, tracks performance data, and synchronizes every element of your campaigns across platforms. In essence, setup is not just technical — it's strategic. Your system will either empower your marketing to scale or limit it to manual inefficiency.

Begin by identifying the platforms you actively use for advertising. For most businesses, this includes Facebook, Instagram, YouTube, TikTok, and LinkedIn. Each of these has its own ad manager, metrics, and data structure. The goal is to unify them into one dashboard — the AI control center. This can be achieved using advanced tools like **AdCreative.ai**, **HubSpot Marketing Hub**, **Hootsuite AI**, **Sprinklr**, or **Metricool**. These systems integrate all platforms via API connections, enabling real-time data flow and automated adjustments. Once you connect your accounts, your AI dashboard becomes the heart of your marketing engine —

pulling audience insights, cost data, engagement rates, and conversion tracking into a unified, intelligent interface.

Account integration is just the beginning. The next phase involves **data calibration** – teaching your AI what matters most to your brand. The more data you feed it, the smarter it becomes. Import past campaigns, existing audiences, top-performing creatives, and conversion metrics. AI thrives on patterns; by giving it a full picture of your historical data, it learns what worked and what didn't. This process creates a baseline model that informs every future optimization. If your system notices that image-based ads perform better on Instagram while short vertical videos dominate TikTok, it will automatically adapt your future content to fit those behavioral insights.

Once your integrations are complete, it's time to define your **goals and KPIs** (Key Performance Indicators). AI cannot optimize what it doesn't understand. Decide what success looks like – is it lead generation, e-commerce sales, engagement, or brand awareness? Each goal will require different data tracking and automation settings. For instance, a conversion-focused campaign might rely heavily on AI pixel tracking, while a brand-awareness campaign uses reach and engagement algorithms. In your AI dashboard, create labeled campaigns with clear objectives. This allows your system to segment performance data intelligently and continuously learn which campaigns yield the highest returns for specific goals.

The next step is **creative automation** – the backbone of AI marketing efficiency. Most modern AI ad platforms come with tools that generate headlines, captions, and even visuals automatically based on brand tone and campaign intent. By using generative AI copywriting and design tools, you can produce dozens of ad variations in minutes. This doesn't replace creativity; it multiplies it. You can test 20 ideas where before you tested two. Then, your AI manager will automatically test, measure, and scale the winners while pausing the rest. This is how businesses achieve exponential ROI growth – not by working harder, but by working smarter with AI's help.

Scheduling automation follows naturally. AI schedulers such as **Buffer AI**, **Later**, or **Hootsuite Smart Scheduling** use predictive engagement data to determine when your audience is most active. Instead of guessing posting times or relying on outdated rules like "best time to post is 6 p.m.," AI scheduling tools calculate the ideal posting moment per platform, per audience segment, per content type. Once established, your campaigns will run automatically at the most profitable times, boosting engagement and lowering costs without manual input.

Finally, you'll configure **AI analytics and reporting**. This feature turns raw data into actionable insights. AI systems generate cross-platform reports that reveal exactly where your money is working hardest. They'll identify underperforming ads, detect hidden trends, and forecast future outcomes using predictive modeling. With a well-set system, you'll be able to see not only what's happening now but what will likely happen next week or next month. That level of foresight turns ordinary marketers into data-driven strategists.

Setting up your AI ad system is not about connecting a few apps and hoping for automation — it's about designing a self-learning ecosystem. Each platform you connect becomes a neuron in your marketing brain. As data circulates through it, the AI learns, adapts, and evolves. The earlier you begin, the faster your system matures and the more intelligent your future campaigns become. Once complete, you'll have built the central nervous system of your digital empire — one that operates 24/7, scales globally, and requires minimal supervision while delivering extraordinary results.

Jason's Creative Generator

Jason was the founder of a small e-commerce brand that sold eco-friendly apparel. He had built everything himself — from the Shopify website to the Facebook ads. But despite his best efforts, managing campaigns across multiple platforms was becoming a nightmare. He would spend hours every night juggling dashboards, trying to understand why TikTok was performing better than Instagram, and why his YouTube ads weren't converting. Every platform told a different story, and the more data he collected, the less clarity he had. He knew there had to be a smarter way.

One evening, while listening to a podcast about AI in marketing, Jason heard an interview with a founder who had automated her entire ad ecosystem. She described how her system connected Facebook, Instagram, TikTok, and Google Ads into one AI dashboard that analyzed everything for her – identifying what worked, predicting what didn't, and automatically reallocating budgets for maximum ROI. Jason paused the episode and scribbled notes furiously. This was exactly what he needed.

The next morning, he signed up for a free trial of an AI marketing platform. The onboarding wizard walked him through each connection: Facebook Ads Manager, TikTok Ads, YouTube Studio, and Google Analytics. Within an hour, the system had pulled in every campaign he'd ever run. The dashboard lit up like a brain – colorful graphs and data streams flowed in real time. For the first time, he saw his entire marketing universe on one screen.

Then came the real magic. The AI began analyzing his past campaigns, learning from his mistakes and successes. It quickly discovered that Jason's short, upbeat TikTok clips outperformed his static Instagram posts by 340%. It also revealed that his best-performing Facebook ads featured customers in real environments rather than studio shots. The system automatically generated recommendations: "Increase budget for TikTok short videos," "Recreate lifestyle images for Facebook," and "Pause YouTube campaigns with low view-through rates." It was like having a full-time marketing strategist on call — except this one never slept.

Over the next week, Jason followed the AI's advice. He connected Canva to the system's creative generator and used AI copywriting prompts to produce 20 ad captions optimized for his top audiences. He then activated the scheduler, which automatically selected the best posting times for each platform based on audience engagement history. The first week's results stunned him. His ad spend dropped by 18%, while conversions increased by nearly 40%. He had achieved more progress in seven days of automation than in the past six months of manual effort.

Within a month, Jason's system had evolved into something extraordinary. His AI dashboard was running multiple campaigns simultaneously — launching new ads, adjusting budgets, and producing daily performance reports without any human input. Each morning, he would open his laptop and review the AI's recommendations over coffee. It felt less like management and more like collaboration — as though he and his digital assistant were running the business together. He began spending his evenings not on spreadsheets, but on creative brainstorming sessions — dreaming up new product videos and brand stories that the AI could help bring to life.

As sales climbed, Jason finally understood the deeper purpose of automation. It wasn't just about saving time; it was about multiplying capability. His one-person brand now operated like a professional marketing agency. When friends asked how he was keeping up, he simply smiled and said, "I stopped trying to do everything myself — now I let the system do the thinking."

By the end of the year, Jason's company had expanded internationally, his customer base had tripled, and his advertising ran 24/7 — flawlessly, efficiently, and intelligently. What began as an overwhelming mix of dashboards and spreadsheets had transformed into a smooth, self-learning marketing machine. And every time he looked at the analytics report that arrived automatically in his inbox, Jason couldn't help but think: this is what the future of business feels like — freedom powered by intelligence.

Chapter 3: Automating Ad Creation and Creative Testing With AI

The creative process has always been the heart of advertising. In the past, crafting an ad required brainstorming sessions, endless revisions, and expensive creative teams to test multiple versions of visuals and copy. Today, artificial intelligence has revolutionized that process. AI doesn't just assist in ad creation—it drives it. From generating headlines to designing images, from crafting emotionally resonant hooks to testing hundreds of ad combinations simultaneously, AI has turned what was once a slow, expensive process into a high-speed, data-driven engine of innovation.

The most powerful aspect of AI-driven ad creation lies in its ability to blend creativity with data science. Traditional creative decisions relied on intuition—what "looked good" or "sounded catchy." Now, AI combines aesthetic understanding with predictive analytics. It analyzes previous ad performance, audience behavior, engagement rates, and emotional responses to craft content that has the highest probability of success. It's like hiring a creative director who also happens to be a data scientist—one who knows exactly which combination of tone, color, and message resonates best with your audience.

Modern AI tools such as **AdCreative.ai**, **Canva Magic**

Studio, **Copy.ai**, and **ChatGPT for Ads** allow marketers to generate endless variations of ad creatives in seconds. You can input a short description of your product, and the AI will generate multiple headlines, captions, call-to-actions, and visual layouts designed for specific platforms. For example, it might create a playful tone for TikTok, a professional tone for LinkedIn, and a high-energy format for YouTube—all from the same message. This versatility ensures that your brand remains consistent yet adaptive to each audience and platform.

Once your creatives are generated, the next critical step is **automated testing**. In traditional marketing, A/B testing meant running two or three variations of an ad and manually analyzing results over several days or weeks. AI has transformed that into **multivariate testing**, where dozens or even hundreds of variations are launched simultaneously. The system continuously tracks engagement, conversions, watch time, and click-through rates, then uses machine learning algorithms to automatically eliminate poor performers while scaling the winning versions. This process ensures that your ad budget is always spent on the best possible creative combinations.

AI creative testing doesn't stop at performance—it also measures **emotional resonance**. Advanced platforms now use **computer vision** and **natural language processing** to analyze how real people react to your visuals and text. They detect facial expressions, tone sentiment, and engagement time, correlating those patterns with conversions. For example, if the AI learns that your audience responds more positively to smiling faces or bright backgrounds, it automatically prioritizes those creative styles in future campaigns. This real-time feedback loop replaces guesswork with precision marketing.

Another key benefit is **speed and scalability**. AI creative tools can produce and test in days what used to take months. This means marketers can keep up with fast-changing trends and platform algorithms. When a new TikTok trend emerges or Meta updates its ad structure, your AI system can adapt immediately—generating new creatives optimized for that environment. This agility ensures that your brand stays relevant and competitive in the constantly shifting landscape of social media advertising.

But automation alone isn't enough. The real secret lies in **human oversight and creative direction**. While AI can create, test, and optimize, it still needs human vision to define brand identity, tone, and emotional depth. Successful marketers learn how to guide AI by feeding it the right prompts, choosing the right data sets, and interpreting insights. Think of AI as a powerful co-pilot—it can navigate the storm, but you must set the destination. Together, you can produce ad campaigns that are not only efficient but also authentically connected to your brand story.

As you integrate AI creative tools into your workflow, establish a structured process: first, define your core message and audience; second, use AI to generate creative variations; third, run automated testing cycles; fourth, analyze AI-driven insights; and finally, refine your creative strategy based on real data. This iterative loop turns every campaign into a learning experience, continuously improving your marketing intelligence. Over time, your AI system learns what visual language, tone, and emotional triggers drive your conversions, enabling you to replicate success predictably.

The future of advertising is not about choosing between creativity and technology—it's about merging them. AI transforms the creative process from an art guided by instinct into a science powered by precision. When used effectively, it doesn't replace your creativity; it amplifies it. You become the director of an intelligent creative ecosystem that never sleeps, constantly learns, and relentlessly optimizes. This is how the world's leading brands are achieving consistent, scalable growth—and it's how you can too.

Why Amira's Skin Care Brand Was Struggling

Amira had always considered herself a creative marketer. Her small digital agency had built a reputation for producing clever, emotionally charged campaigns that connected with audiences. But recently, she was feeling overwhelmed. The sheer speed of social media had changed everything. What worked on Instagram one week became outdated the next. Her clients expected daily content, quick results, and measurable ROI. Despite her best efforts, Amira felt like she was running on a treadmill—creating constantly but never catching up.

One afternoon, while preparing for a client meeting, she discovered a new AI creative platform. It promised to generate ad copy, visuals, and even video templates automatically. Skeptical but curious, she uploaded one of her underperforming campaigns—a skincare brand struggling to stand out in a crowded market. Within minutes, the AI analyzed her existing ads, reviewed performance data, and generated twelve new versions of the same campaign. Each variation featured different headlines, colors, and emotional tones. Some emphasized "confidence," others "self-care," and a few focused purely on "scientific results." Amira couldn't believe what she was seeing.

She decided to test the AI's work. Over the next week, she ran all twelve versions using her ad manager's automated testing feature. The results were staggering. One version, featuring a natural photo and a gentle headline—"Love the Skin You're In"—outperformed all others by 310%. The AI had found the perfect emotional resonance her team had missed. It wasn't just about beauty; it was about authenticity. The system automatically paused the weaker ads and shifted more budget toward the winner. Her client's cost per conversion dropped by half in just five days.

Encouraged, Amira dove deeper into the system. She learned how to guide the AI more effectively, feeding it detailed brand information, tone of voice, and visual preferences. Soon, her creative process became faster, smarter, and more strategic. Instead of spending hours brainstorming, she spent minutes refining AI-generated ideas. She began using ChatGPT-based ad copy tools to craft emotionally compelling captions and AI visual platforms like Midjourney and Leonardo to design on-brand imagery. Every campaign became a collaboration between her human creativity and the AI's analytical intelligence.

Then came her biggest client yet: a global fitness brand looking to launch a new product line. Normally, this would require a full creative team and several weeks of development. But with her new AI workflow, Amira completed the first round of campaigns in just two days. The system generated over fifty ad variations, optimized for TikTok, Instagram Reels, and YouTube Shorts. The AI automatically analyzed engagement data every hour, adjusting targeting and visuals in real time. Within a week, the campaign went viral. The client's sales skyrocketed, and Amira's agency gained international recognition.

What surprised her most wasn't just the results—it was how free she felt. Instead of drowning in endless creative pressure, she could finally focus on the bigger picture: brand storytelling, partnerships, and strategy. The AI handled the technical aspects of creative testing and optimization, while she provided the heart and vision. Together, they achieved a balance that no human or machine could accomplish alone.

Months later, Amira looked back on that first campaign and smiled. She realized she had crossed a threshold—from manual marketer to AI-powered creator. Her clients now saw her as a visionary, not just a service provider. She wasn't afraid of automation anymore; she embraced it. Because in truth, AI hadn't replaced her—it had unleashed her. The endless loop of testing, analyzing, and improving became her new creative playground, and with each campaign, her agency grew stronger, smarter, and more profitable.

Amira's story mirrors the evolution of marketing itself.

Creativity will always come from humans, but AI provides the canvas, the brushes, and the infinite colors to paint with. Those who understand how to harness this partnership will not only survive in the digital age—they'll lead it.

Chapter 4: Building Cross-Platform Ad Workflows and Integration Systems

Running ads on a single social network is no longer enough to build a sustainable digital presence. Modern consumers move seamlessly between platforms: they may discover a brand on TikTok, research it on YouTube, follow it on Instagram, and finally make a purchase after seeing a retargeting ad on Facebook or Google. To reach this cross-channel audience effectively, advertisers need **integrated workflows** that connect every stage of the customer journey. Artificial intelligence makes this possible by unifying data, automating coordination, and ensuring consistent messaging across all channels.

A cross-platform workflow begins with **centralized data synchronization**. Instead of treating each platform as a separate silo, your AI system should gather and harmonize data from Meta, Google, TikTok, LinkedIn, and other ad networks into one central hub. This creates what is often called a “single source of truth.” Every click, impression, conversion, and cost is recorded in real time. AI tools such as **HubSpot Marketing Hub**, **Zapier AI**, **Make.com**, or **Sprinklr Unified Ads** automatically pull this data and translate it into comparable metrics. With a unified data foundation, you can evaluate performance holistically, identifying which platforms attract awareness, which drive engagement, and which close sales.

The next step is designing **cross-platform campaign flows**. Think of this as your brand's advertising choreography—each channel plays a distinct role, yet they all move in harmony. For example, a prospect might first see a 10-second awareness ad on TikTok, then be shown an educational YouTube video, followed by a Facebook retargeting ad with a limited-time offer. AI systems can automate this sequencing using behavioral triggers. When a user watches a certain percentage of a video or clicks on a link, the AI automatically moves them to the next phase of the funnel on a different platform. This approach transforms scattered campaigns into a seamless multi-touch experience.

To implement this, you'll need **integration bridges**—automated connections that allow platforms to share data and respond dynamically. Tools like **Meta Pixel**, **Google Tag Manager**, and **LinkedIn Insight Tag** track user actions across sites and feed that information back to your AI dashboard. From there, automations built in Make.com or Zapier route users between campaigns. For example, if someone fills out a lead form on Facebook but doesn't schedule a consultation, the system can instantly trigger a follow-up video ad on YouTube or a reminder message via email. This interconnectivity ensures that no potential customer slips through the cracks.

Automation also allows for **budget fluidity across platforms**. Traditionally, marketers allocated fixed amounts—$500 for Facebook, $300 for Google, etc.—and adjusted manually at month's end. AI-driven integration changes that model completely. With predictive budget optimization, the system continuously reallocates spending in real time based on performance. If it detects higher conversion rates on TikTok or a sudden surge in engagement on Instagram, it automatically shifts budget from underperforming channels. The result is maximum return on ad spend without constant human monitoring.

Beyond budgeting, AI integration enhances **creative consistency and version control**. With connected systems, your brand messaging, color palette, and tone stay uniform across every ad and platform. The AI can automatically resize images, reformat captions, and translate content for each channel while maintaining brand voice. This prevents the disjointed experiences that often occur when multiple teams manage campaigns separately. In a world where brand trust is built through repetition and coherence, consistent cross-platform messaging is invaluable. The final piece of the puzzle is **analytics and insight integration**. Once your workflows are active, AI dashboards can generate unified performance reports that visualize your entire marketing funnel—from first impression to final sale. You can view engagement timelines, cross-channel attribution paths, and ROI projections. More advanced systems even use predictive modeling to forecast future trends and recommend upcoming campaign adjustments. These insights turn marketing from reactive management into proactive strategy. You no longer guess; you know what to do next.

Building cross-platform ad workflows is more than a technical upgrade—it's a strategic evolution. It reflects the way real people behave online: fluidly, unpredictably, and across multiple touchpoints. By integrating your systems through AI, you give your brand the ability to follow customers naturally, respond intelligently, and scale efficiently. Once these connections are established, your marketing ecosystem operates like a living organism—self-aware, adaptive, and capable of growing without constant manual input. That's the true power of AI-driven integration.

Lena Finally Connected With Make.com

Lena sat in her office surrounded by glowing monitors, each displaying a different ad dashboard. Her boutique marketing agency had grown quickly, and with growth came chaos.

Facebook campaigns ran separately from Google; TikTok analytics lived in a spreadsheet; YouTube data arrived weekly via email reports. Every morning felt like decoding a dozen different languages. Her clients wanted unified answers—Which ads were working? Which audiences were converting?—but she couldn't see the full picture. It was like trying to conduct an orchestra while each musician played from a different sheet of music.

One night, exhausted and frustrated, Lena decided to overhaul everything. She stayed up researching automation and discovered a case study on AI-driven cross-platform workflows. The concept fascinated her: connect all ad platforms into one central brain that managed data, budgets, and creative consistency automatically. It sounded ambitious, but Lena had reached her breaking point. The next day, she began setting it up.

She started small—integrating Facebook, Instagram, and Google Ads through Make.com. The system linked each platform's API, feeding live performance data into a single dashboard. When she saw the first unified report appear on her screen, Lena felt a rush of relief. For the first time, she could see how a lead discovered on TikTok eventually converted through a retargeting ad on Facebook. Patterns that had once been invisible suddenly came to life before her eyes.

Encouraged, she went further. She connected her clients' CRM systems, email sequences, and website analytics into the same AI network. The automations began to flow: when a lead watched 75% of a YouTube video, the AI triggered an Instagram Story ad offering a free trial. If a customer clicked but didn't buy, the system sent a personalized follow-up email. Within a week, everything was synchronized. Her ads were no longer isolated efforts—they were chapters in a continuous conversation.

The results were immediate. Conversion rates increased, and ad waste plummeted. The AI detected that one client's budget was underperforming on Google but thriving on TikTok, so it automatically reallocated funds mid-campaign. Another client's Facebook ads were generating high engagement but low conversions, prompting the AI to launch complementary retargeting ads on Instagram that closed the loop. Lena didn't have to intervene; the system was learning, thinking, and optimizing on its own.

Her clients were amazed. During meetings, Lena could show them dynamic reports that tracked every touchpoint of a customer's journey. They watched animated dashboards reveal how awareness ads led to consideration videos and, eventually, purchases. For the first time, marketing made complete sense—not as isolated metrics, but as a living ecosystem. "It's like watching the internet breathe," one client said, marveling at the data visualization.

Freed from constant dashboard management, Lena had time to focus on creative direction and long-term strategy. She collaborated with her AI system the way a pilot works with autopilot—setting goals, adjusting course, and letting the machine handle the technical precision. Her agency's reputation soared, and new clients flooded in. The once-chaotic environment now operated like a finely tuned symphony of automation and insight.

Months later, Lena reflected on the transformation. What had started as a desperate attempt to bring order to her workload had become the foundation of a scalable business model. Her AI-driven workflows didn't just manage ads; they managed growth. Her team could now launch multi-channel campaigns in days instead of weeks, all synchronized and data-driven. She realized she was no longer chasing algorithms—she was orchestrating them.

And perhaps the most rewarding part was the sense of clarity. No more scattered spreadsheets, no more guessing. Every click, every conversion, every dollar had a purpose and a place. Lena's integrated system had become the silent partner behind her agency's success—an invisible network of intelligence ensuring that every campaign, no matter the platform, played in perfect harmony.

Chapter 5: AI-Driven Audience Targeting and Personalization

Audience targeting used to mean broad demographics – age, gender, location, or interests. But today's digital ecosystem demands precision. Consumers expect ads that feel personal, timely, and relevant to their current needs. Artificial intelligence has become the driving force behind this new era of hyper-personalized marketing. Through predictive analytics, behavioral modeling, and real-time data interpretation, AI can not only find your ideal customers but also anticipate what they want before they do. This is the evolution from mass marketing to **individualized engagement**.

At its core, AI-driven audience targeting begins with **data aggregation**. Every digital action – clicks, watch time, scroll depth, search queries, and even dwell time – becomes a data point. AI systems aggregate these across multiple platforms, creating detailed behavioral profiles far beyond simple demographics. Instead of "women aged 30 to 40 in Florida," the AI identifies micro-segments such as "women who engage with eco-friendly products, watch short fitness videos at night, and respond to motivational messaging." These patterns allow advertisers to speak directly to intent, not identity.

The next stage is **predictive modeling**. Machine-learning algorithms examine historical data and forecast future actions. If a user interacts with specific types of content, the system predicts their next likely step — perhaps downloading a guide, visiting a product page, or watching a testimonial. These predictive insights power proactive marketing. Rather than reacting to what customers do, your campaigns anticipate their journey and place the right message in front of them at exactly the right moment. AI converts guesswork into foresight.

Personalization extends beyond targeting; it permeates **creative customization**. AI tools like Persado, Phrasee, and Copy.ai can generate thousands of message variations tailored to specific emotional triggers or psychographic profiles. The system tests different tones — empathy, authority, humor, or urgency — to determine which resonates with each audience cluster. Visual personalization platforms like Canva AI and Dynamic Creative Optimization (DCO) systems automatically adjust imagery, colors, and layouts depending on user preferences. One viewer might see a calm pastel ad emphasizing comfort, while another sees a bold design focused on ambition. Both experiences align perfectly with individual intent.

AI also enables **cross-channel retargeting** that feels seamless rather than invasive. When integrated properly, an AI system recognizes a user's interaction on one platform and continues the conversation elsewhere. For example, if someone clicks an Instagram ad but doesn't purchase, the AI may show them a YouTube video explaining the product's benefits, followed by a personalized email offering a discount. Each message feels contextual – a continuation of a story rather than a repetition of an ad. This consistency builds trust and dramatically improves conversion rates.

Data privacy remains a crucial consideration. As regulations evolve, AI platforms must comply with GDPR, CCPA, and other regional privacy laws. Responsible advertisers embrace **ethical personalization**, using first-party and consent-based data. Fortunately, AI excels at anonymized pattern recognition. It doesn't need names or emails to detect behavior trends; it relies on aggregated signals. This ensures personalization without compromising privacy, strengthening consumer confidence and brand credibility.

The final piece of the puzzle is **real-time adaptation**. Traditional campaigns used static targeting – once launched, parameters rarely changed. AI systems operate dynamically. They constantly analyze new data streams, adjusting audiences, creatives, and budgets automatically. If a campaign suddenly performs better with a new audience cluster, the AI expands its reach; if engagement drops, it pivots instantly. This agility transforms marketing into a living, breathing organism that evolves alongside audience behavior.

The result of this evolution is profound. AI turns data into empathy. It allows brands to treat millions of people not as numbers but as individuals with unique preferences and emotions. This isn't just better marketing — it's better communication. When every ad feels relevant, customers stop seeing them as interruptions and start perceiving them as helpful recommendations. Mastering AI-driven targeting and personalization means mastering connection at scale — the ultimate goal of modern marketing.

The AI System That Discovered Sophie

Sophie managed marketing for a growing online wellness brand. Her company sold supplements and digital fitness programs, but her ads felt invisible. Despite beautiful designs and thoughtful copy, engagement was flat. "Maybe we're targeting too broadly," she thought as she scanned yet another disappointing report. She knew her products helped thousands of people, yet her message wasn't reaching the right ones.

One morning, she attended a virtual summit on AI in advertising. A speaker demonstrated how machine learning could analyze not just who interacted with ads, but why. The example stunned her: an AI system had discovered that customers who listened to late-night meditation playlists were more likely to purchase wellness subscriptions within three days. Sophie realized her current approach — segmenting only by age and gender — was prehistoric compared to what was possible. She decided to rebuild everything from scratch.

She subscribed to an AI-powered targeting platform that integrated directly with her social accounts. The setup took hours, not days. As soon as she uploaded past campaign data, the system began mapping behavioral patterns. Within minutes, it identified hidden micro-audiences she had never noticed — people who engaged with self-improvement podcasts, read personal-growth blogs, and preferred mobile video ads over static images. It also detected emotional triggers that worked best for each group: empowerment for one, serenity for another.

When the new campaign launched, it felt like magic. Each ad variation adjusted automatically to match its viewer. Someone scrolling late at night saw a calm blue ad with the message, *"Unwind and recharge before tomorrow begins."* Morning viewers saw brighter visuals and the line, *"Start strong. Fuel your energy naturally."* Even the call-to-action buttons shifted colors based on predicted emotional response. Sophie watched engagement rates climb like never before.

Within two weeks, the AI had fine-tuned the entire funnel. It realized that users who watched more than half of a short educational video were 70 percent more likely to convert. The system began prioritizing those viewers across platforms, retargeting them with personalized follow-ups. The experience felt conversational — as if the brand were reading customers' minds, offering help exactly when they needed it. Sales doubled, cost-per-lead dropped by nearly 50 percent, and customer satisfaction surveys skyrocketed.

But the real transformation came from what Sophie learned about her audience. The AI's insights revealed motivations that no survey had ever captured — stress relief, confidence, balance. She used those findings to reshape her brand's tone, website, and email content. Her marketing no longer revolved around products; it revolved around people. Every campaign told a story of empowerment and well-being, supported by data yet driven by empathy.

Months later, Sophie reflected on the shift. Before AI, she had felt like a marketer shouting into a void. Now, she was having genuine conversations with her customers — thousands of them at once, yet each one unique. Her AI targeting system had become more than a tool; it was a bridge between human understanding and machine intelligence. The technology didn't just help her sell more; it helped her connect more deeply.

For Sophie, and for every marketer embracing personalization, the lesson was clear: when data meets empathy, marketing becomes meaningful. And in a world overflowing with noise, meaning is the ultimate competitive advantage.

Chapter 6: AI Copywriting and Ad Messaging Optimization

In advertising, words are everything. The right headline can stop a scroll, the right caption can spark curiosity, and the right call-to-action can turn interest into conversion. But finding those right words has traditionally been a painstaking process of trial, intuition, and endless revision. Now, with the rise of artificial intelligence, copywriting has entered a new era—one of speed, precision, and data-backed creativity. AI copywriting tools don't just write faster; they write smarter. They analyze performance data, emotional tone, and user behavior to craft messages that connect deeply with specific audiences at the perfect time.

At its foundation, **AI copywriting** relies on natural language processing (NLP), a branch of AI that enables machines to understand and generate human language. These systems are trained on billions of data points—ads, blog posts, emails, and conversations—to learn not only what people say but how they respond emotionally. When used strategically, AI becomes more than a writing assistant—it becomes a conversion scientist. It studies what words engage, what phrases persuade, and what structures trigger action. Over time, it develops a language model tailored to your brand's unique tone and goals.

The first step to using AI copywriting effectively is defining your **brand voice**. Even the most advanced algorithms require clear direction. Do you want your tone to be friendly, confident, luxurious, or motivational? Should your copy inspire trust, excitement, or exclusivity? Feeding your AI with detailed examples helps it generate consistent, on-brand messaging across every platform. Tools like **ChatGPT, Jasper, Copy.ai, and Writesonic** allow for customizable tone settings and memory features that help maintain brand coherence over time. Once calibrated, your AI becomes fluent in your style—creating text that feels personal, consistent, and authentically human.

Next comes **message optimization through data feedback**. Every ad campaign produces metrics—click-through rates, watch time, engagement ratios, conversion percentages. AI systems ingest these results, analyze them, and adjust future messaging accordingly. For instance, if the AI notices that emotionally charged phrases outperform logical ones in your audience segment, it will naturally generate more empathy-driven copy. If short headlines convert better than long-form descriptions, it will optimize length automatically. This closed feedback loop turns your ad copywriting into a self-learning process that improves with every campaign.

Another breakthrough lies in **dynamic message personalization**. Instead of one-size-fits-all copy, AI allows each user to experience unique wording depending on their behavior or interests. For example, an e-commerce visitor who browsed athletic shoes might see "Run Faster. Go Further." while someone interested in casual sneakers sees "Walk Your Way. Stay Stylish." The AI determines which emotional trigger—performance, style, comfort, or freedom—drives the highest likelihood of purchase. This hyper-personalized messaging drastically boosts engagement and conversion because it mirrors how real conversations work: adaptive, contextual, and emotionally intelligent.

AI copywriting also streamlines **testing and iteration**. Previously, marketers could test two or three headline variations at a time. Now, AI can generate hundreds, each with subtle variations in tone, phrasing, or emotional appeal. It automatically distributes and analyzes performance, identifying top performers within hours instead of weeks. The system doesn't just declare winners—it studies why they won, building predictive linguistic models for future campaigns. This is the scientific evolution of persuasion, where every word is measurable and every improvement is scalable.

Yet, even with automation, human creativity remains essential. AI can simulate voice, rhythm, and structure, but only humans can craft emotional narratives that move hearts. The best results come from collaboration. Let the AI draft dozens of variations—then refine, combine, and elevate them with your creative intuition. AI copywriting is not about outsourcing creativity; it's about amplifying it. It eliminates writer's block, speeds up ideation, and provides endless inspiration, allowing marketers to focus on storytelling and emotional resonance rather than repetitive text generation.

Finally, the integration of **sentiment analysis** has made messaging optimization more intelligent than ever. AI systems can analyze not only engagement rates but also how people feel about your message. Using NLP models, they detect whether a comment, review, or response expresses joy, confusion, anger, or interest. They then adjust your ad tone accordingly. This feedback allows brands to evolve in real time, ensuring every message aligns with audience sentiment and cultural mood.

When implemented correctly, AI copywriting becomes your creative accelerator and strategist in one. It delivers messages that are not just relevant but magnetic—crafted with precision, tested with data, and enhanced through emotional intelligence. The combination of art and algorithm creates something extraordinary: communication that feels deeply human, yet powered by machine-level insight.

Your Copy Doesn't Fail Because It's Bad

When Daniel launched his online education business, he quickly discovered how hard it was to write ad copy that truly connected. He tried everything—long descriptions, clever headlines, emotional storytelling—but nothing consistently performed. Each week, he would tweak words, adjust CTAs, and rewrite entire campaigns, yet results barely changed. "Maybe I'm just not a good copywriter," he told himself. But deep down, he knew the problem wasn't his creativity—it was the lack of data guiding it.

One evening, while watching a webinar about AI marketing, Daniel heard a speaker mention something that clicked instantly: "Your copy doesn't fail because it's bad—it fails because it's uninformed." The presenter demonstrated how AI could write hundreds of data-backed variations, test them automatically, and refine them based on real human response. Daniel was intrigued. Within minutes, he signed up for an AI copywriting platform and connected it to his ad accounts.

He started small, giving the AI a simple prompt: *"Write Facebook ads for my course that helps beginners create and sell digital products."* In seconds, the system generated fifteen different headlines. Some were direct—"Turn Your Ideas Into Income in 10 Days." Others were emotional—"Create Once, Earn Forever." One was bold: *"Quit Guessing. Start Creating."* Daniel selected his favorites and launched a test campaign. The next day, the AI reported that emotional headlines outperformed logical ones by 63%. It automatically generated new variations using emotional tones—and engagement skyrocketed.

Encouraged, Daniel pushed further. He asked the AI to rewrite captions for Instagram Reels, tailoring tone to different personality types. One set spoke to dreamers; another targeted analytical thinkers. Each audience segment received its own voice and phrasing. The AI even adjusted CTAs dynamically: creatives saw "Bring Your Vision to Life," while entrepreneurs saw "Build Your Next Stream of Income." The difference was astonishing. His click-through rates doubled, cost-per-click dropped, and more importantly, comments poured in from people saying, "It feels like you're talking directly to me."

Over the next few weeks, Daniel's workflow changed completely. Instead of agonizing over every sentence, he became a strategist. He focused on big-picture storytelling while his AI handled linguistic precision. He would enter a prompt, receive dozens of options, and then blend the best lines into powerful, emotionally layered campaigns. His confidence grew, not because AI replaced him, but because it revealed how his words could truly connect. He finally understood his audience–not as abstract data points, but as people moved by emotions, dreams, and aspirations. Then came his breakthrough moment. Daniel used sentiment analysis tools integrated into his AI system to analyze thousands of comments and reactions. He discovered patterns: people felt inspired but occasionally skeptical about time commitment. So, the AI helped him craft new messaging around "fast wins" and "real progress in just minutes a day." Conversions surged again. For the first time, Daniel's messaging wasn't just persuasive–it was empathetic, addressing real concerns before customers even voiced them.

Months later, Daniel's business had tripled in revenue. His ads no longer felt like ads–they felt like personal invitations. He often joked that his AI tool was his "silent copywriter," but in truth, it had become his creative partner. He would brainstorm ideas late at night, feeding them into the system, and wake up to dozens of perfectly written, ready-to-test variations. The process reignited his passion for marketing because it transformed writing from a guessing game into an exciting collaboration.

Looking back, Daniel realized something profound. AI hadn't taken over his voice–it had amplified it. It helped him express his ideas more clearly, test them more intelligently, and connect with more people than ever before. What once took weeks of writing and revising now happened in hours, and every message carried precision born of data and empathy. The technology didn't make him less human—it helped him speak to humans better.

In Daniel's journey lies a lesson for every modern marketer: the future of copywriting isn't automation alone—it's collaboration. When human creativity meets machine intelligence, words stop being just text on a screen; they become living connections, engineered to inspire action and emotion at once.

Chapter 7: AI-Enhanced Ad Budgeting and ROI Optimization

Budgeting used to be the part of advertising that felt most like gambling. Marketers would plan budgets at the start of the month, distribute funds across platforms based on instinct or past experience, and hope for the best. The problem was that the digital landscape changed too fast for static planning. What worked yesterday might fail tomorrow. Artificial intelligence has solved that problem by turning budgeting from guesswork into a living, learning system that reacts to performance in real time.

AI-enhanced budgeting begins with **data integration and predictive modeling**. Every platform—Meta, Google, TikTok, YouTube—produces a constant stream of performance metrics: cost-per-click, impressions, view-through rates, conversions, and engagement depth. AI algorithms ingest these data sets simultaneously, detecting patterns that reveal not only which ads are performing now but which will likely perform tomorrow. These insights power **predictive budget allocation**, where funds shift dynamically toward campaigns expected to yield the highest ROI.

The process starts by defining clear **ROI objectives**. Are you optimizing for lead volume, purchase conversions, or lifetime customer value? Once set, your AI uses reinforcement learning to adjust spend based on live results. It may increase the budget for a top-performing ad while instantly pausing another that's losing momentum. Some systems even simulate "what-if" scenarios before making changes, testing outcomes virtually before committing real dollars. The result is precision spending: not a dollar wasted, not an opportunity missed.

Another key element is **cross-platform fluidity**. Traditional ad managers treat budgets as silos—$1,000 for Meta, $500 for YouTube, and so on. AI breaks those walls. It views all campaigns as parts of a single ecosystem. If YouTube views start converting better than Instagram clicks, the AI automatically shifts funds across platforms to follow profitability. This flexibility is impossible for manual teams to maintain at scale, but for algorithms, it's instantaneous. Over time, this creates an adaptive financial rhythm that always aligns spend with performance.

Beyond allocation, AI enhances **bid strategy optimization**. Instead of setting manual bids or relying on broad automated bidding options, machine-learning models evaluate thousands of micro-factors in real time—audience intent, device type, time of day, and competitor activity—to calculate the optimal bid for each impression. These systems use continuous feedback loops to learn which bid levels produce the best conversion cost and quality. Marketers no longer chase trends—they let data dictate every penny's path.

Transparency has also improved. AI dashboards now visualize ROI in ways that humans can interpret easily. They translate raw data into visual maps of spend efficiency, showing which campaigns are generating returns and which are underperforming. Advanced systems like **Revealbot, Adzooma, and Madgicx** even provide "profitability heatmaps," allowing marketers to see precisely where each dollar goes and how it multiplies. This clarity empowers smarter decisions and confidence in scaling budgets.

Crucially, AI doesn't just measure *financial* ROI—it measures *strategic* ROI. It can assess how ad spending contributes to long-term brand growth, customer retention, and audience expansion. By merging transactional data with behavioral analytics, it reveals insights such as, "This campaign produces fewer sales now but brings in the most loyal customers later." That kind of intelligence helps brands invest for sustainability, not just short-term gain.

The final frontier is **autonomous budget optimization**, where AI systems manage spend end-to-end with minimal human intervention. These platforms run continuous micro-tests, reallocating budgets hourly or even minute-by-minute based on market dynamics. As privacy laws restrict tracking and cookie data, these systems use anonymized contextual signals—engagement trends, sentiment shifts, and predictive demographics—to maintain accuracy without violating compliance.

When marketers adopt AI-driven budgeting, they gain the ultimate advantage: foresight. Instead of reacting to data after campaigns end, they shape outcomes as they happen. The difference between a traditional ad manager and an AI-powered one is like navigating with a paper map versus GPS. The destination is the same—profit—but AI ensures you reach it faster, cheaper, and more reliably. In this new paradigm, success isn't about how much you spend—it's about how intelligently your system learns to spend for you.

Priya Turns to Revealbot for Help

For years, Priya had run her digital-marketing agency the old-fashioned way. Each month began with spreadsheets, estimates, and debates over how to divide ad spend. Facebook usually got the largest share, Google Ads came second, and whatever was left went to Instagram or TikTok. She based her decisions on gut feeling and experience—and while her instincts were good, the results were unpredictable. Some months brought impressive profits; others barely broke even. She knew something had to change.

One afternoon, while scrolling through an industry forum, she came across a case study titled *"How AI Cut Ad Waste by 47% in 30 Days."* The article described a company using real-time budget optimization powered by machine learning. Intrigued, Priya decided to experiment. She integrated an AI platform called **Revealbot** into her agency's Meta and Google ad accounts, feeding it two years of historical performance data. Overnight, the system began analyzing tens of thousands of past campaigns—identifying trends she had never noticed.

By morning, the dashboard displayed its first recommendation: reallocate 25% of her Meta budget to YouTube for one particular client. At first, Priya hesitated. YouTube hadn't been a major focus for that account. But the AI predicted a 34% increase in conversion value if she made the switch. Trusting the data, she approved the change. Within three days, conversions doubled. The AI had spotted a pattern she'd missed entirely: the client's target demographic spent more time watching tutorial videos than scrolling social feeds.

From that moment, Priya was hooked. She connected every client account, allowing the AI to manage budgets dynamically. It ran hourly adjustments, pulling spend from ads with rising costs and redirecting it toward those showing stronger ROI. It even paused campaigns automatically when market conditions shifted, saving thousands of dollars each month. For the first time, her budget reports showed not chaos but harmony—numbers flowing like a perfectly tuned symphony of data and profit.

The true revelation came when she examined the system's cross-platform behavior. Late one Friday, she noticed that ad spend on Instagram had dropped sharply while TikTok's had risen. Concerned, she opened the AI's reasoning log. It explained that engagement on Instagram had fallen by 19% in the past 48 hours, while TikTok conversions were surging due to a viral challenge relevant to her client's product. The AI had automatically shifted budget in real time to ride the wave. By Monday, sales were up 60%. Priya realized no human could have reacted that fast.

Her clients were astonished. During presentations, she showed them visual dashboards mapping every dollar to measurable results. They could see precisely where their investments went and why. One client said, "It feels like watching my money think for itself." The transparency built trust, and referrals poured in. What used to take an entire department to analyze, the AI accomplished overnight.

Months later, Priya's agency had scaled beyond what she thought possible. Her new motto became "spend intelligently, not excessively." She now viewed budgets not as limits but as living resources that adapted and evolved. Her nights were no longer filled with spreadsheet anxiety. Instead, she reviewed AI insights over coffee each morning, adjusting only the high-level strategy while the system fine-tuned the details.

The transformation went deeper than profit. Priya felt liberated. She wasn't just managing campaigns—she was orchestrating intelligence. Her AI partner wasn't replacing her expertise; it was amplifying it. Together, they achieved balance between creativity and analytics, intuition and precision. When people asked how she managed such consistent growth, she smiled and said, "I stopped spending money. I started investing with intelligence."

And that, she realized, was the essence of modern advertising: not more budget, but smarter budget. In a world where algorithms predict tomorrow's winners today, success belongs to those who let intelligence—not instinct—guide every dollar.

Chapter 8: AI-Powered Retargeting and Conversion Optimization

In the world of digital advertising, few strategies are as powerful—and as misunderstood—as retargeting. Most people who visit a website or interact with an ad don't convert on their first encounter. They may browse, click, or even add items to a cart, but then they disappear into the noise of the internet. Traditional retargeting attempted to bring these users back through repetitive ads, often annoying them instead of inspiring action. Today, **AI-powered retargeting** has changed everything. Using machine learning, behavioral prediction, and contextual analysis, advertisers can now re-engage audiences intelligently, ethically, and profitably.

AI retargeting begins with **audience segmentation through behavioral intelligence**. Instead of lumping all visitors into a single retargeting list, machine learning systems categorize them by intent and readiness to buy. For example, someone who watched a product demo video but didn't purchase might be tagged as "high intent but needs reassurance," while another who viewed multiple product categories may be labeled "browsing and comparing." Each segment receives customized follow-up messaging aligned with its stage in the buyer's journey. The result is a campaign that feels personalized, not repetitive.

The next layer is **predictive retargeting**, where algorithms analyze data across thousands of interactions to forecast which prospects are most likely to convert. These predictions allow marketers to prioritize high-probability leads and allocate more budget toward them, while reducing spend on disengaged users. Platforms like **Google Ads Smart Bidding**, **Meta Advantage+**, and **Criteo AI** already use this principle, automatically bidding higher for users with stronger behavioral signals. Predictive models also identify when to re-engage a user and when to stop—avoiding ad fatigue and preserving brand goodwill.

AI also enhances **creative sequencing**, one of the most underrated yet crucial aspects of retargeting. Traditional ads often show the same image or video repeatedly. AI systems, however, deliver dynamic creative sequences that evolve based on user behavior. If a visitor views a video ad but doesn't click, the next ad they see might feature testimonials or FAQs to address objections. If they visit a pricing page but abandon it, the system may serve an incentive-driven ad—like a discount or free trial offer. This logical storytelling approach transforms retargeting from an annoyance into a conversation.

An equally important function is **contextual timing**

optimization. AI analyzes when users are most receptive to engagement, based on device usage patterns, session duration, and daily routines. It might learn that a specific user tends to click ads late at night or during commute hours and schedule accordingly. This level of timing precision drastically improves click-through and conversion rates because it aligns with natural human behavior rather than arbitrary posting schedules.

AI-powered systems also employ **cross-channel retargeting**, connecting interactions across devices and platforms. A potential customer who interacts with an Instagram video might later see a follow-up ad on YouTube or a personalized email reminder. This continuity builds trust and keeps the brand top of mind without feeling invasive. By merging data from multiple touchpoints, AI creates a holistic user journey that feels organic and intelligently guided.

Finally, **conversion optimization** is where everything comes together. Once users click through retargeted ads, AI continues to analyze on-site behavior to improve landing page performance. Heatmaps, scroll-depth tracking, and engagement analytics feed back into the algorithm, revealing which headlines, buttons, or images influence conversions most. Over time, the system refines both the ad experience and the landing experience simultaneously—creating a feedback loop that continuously increases return on investment.

AI-powered retargeting isn't just about recovering lost traffic—it's about understanding and guiding human behavior with empathy and precision. By showing the right message to the right person at the right time, AI converts hesitation into confidence and curiosity into action. The result is not only more sales but also stronger brand relationships built on relevance and respect. When marketers master this technology, retargeting ceases to feel like chasing prospects and starts to feel like serving them exactly what they need, when they need it most.

The AI That Categorized

Elena owned an online furniture store that sold eco-friendly pieces crafted from reclaimed wood. Her website traffic was strong—thousands of visitors every week—but sales lagged behind. Most users browsed, added items to their cart, and disappeared. She tried traditional retargeting campaigns, showing the same "Come Back and Save 10%" ad to everyone who left the site. The results were disappointing. People saw the ad too many times, ignored it, and some even hid it from their feeds. "It feels like we're stalking our customers," she told her team. She knew she needed a smarter, more human approach.

One day, during a webinar about AI in e-commerce, Elena heard about machine-learning-driven retargeting. The presenter explained how AI could analyze each user's journey and deliver personalized follow-ups that addressed their specific motivations. It sounded exactly like what she'd been missing—intelligence and empathy combined. The next day, she implemented an AI retargeting platform and connected it to her Shopify store, Meta ads, and email system.

Within hours, the AI began categorizing her visitors. It identified five major behavioral groups: "window shoppers," "cart abandoners," "high-value browsers," "returning customers," and "researchers." Each group received different messaging. For instance, window shoppers saw beautiful lifestyle ads showcasing room makeovers, while cart abandoners received short video testimonials from happy customers discussing product quality and easy delivery. For high-value browsers, the AI recommended follow-ups emphasizing eco-impact and sustainability.

The transformation was immediate. Instead of bombarding people with the same discount ad, her campaigns now told evolving stories. If someone had viewed a coffee table but didn't purchase, they later saw a video showing how that table was built from recycled oak—followed by an ad offering free shipping. If another user spent time reading reviews, the AI showed a carousel of five-star testimonials. Every interaction felt natural, like a helpful reminder rather than a pushy sales pitch.

But the real magic happened in timing. The AI learned when each customer segment was most responsive. Some preferred early morning browsing; others engaged late at night. The system automatically adjusted ad delivery to match these patterns. Elena noticed that click-through rates increased by over 60%, and conversions nearly doubled within the first month. Her advertising felt alive—responsive, thoughtful, and fluid.

What impressed her most was how the AI handled disengagement. If someone ignored several ads, the system simply stopped targeting them and replaced retargeting efforts with lookalike audiences modeled after past converters. This respectful restraint kept her brand reputation strong. Customers began commenting on her ads—not to complain, but to thank her for her company's unique, meaningful marketing. They said things like, "I wasn't sure about buying this, but your video convinced me," or "I love that your ads actually make sense!"

By the end of the quarter, Elena's return on ad spend had tripled. Her sales pipeline was no longer random—it was strategic. She began viewing retargeting not as chasing lost customers, but as guiding them through a personalized journey. Every ad became a step in a conversation, leading people naturally toward purchase. The AI didn't just sell more furniture—it helped her brand tell its story in a way that resonated deeply.

Months later, while reviewing her campaign reports, Elena smiled at the shift in mindset. Before AI, she had seen ads as tools to persuade. Now she saw them as tools to serve. The technology allowed her to anticipate her customers' needs before they even expressed them. Her brand no longer felt like a store—it felt like a companion helping people build the homes they dreamed of.

In that realization, Elena understood the future of marketing. AI wasn't just optimizing conversions—it was humanizing them. And that, she knew, was the greatest return on investment of all.

Chapter 9: AI Visual Optimization and Creative Design Systems

Visuals are the soul of digital advertising. In a world dominated by scrolling feeds and short attention spans, images and videos are the first—and often only—chance to capture interest. The average user decides whether to engage with an ad in less than three seconds, making design not just an artistic choice but a strategic one. Artificial intelligence has revolutionized this process, bringing science to creativity. Through machine learning, computer vision, and design automation, AI can now analyze visual performance, predict emotional response, and even generate new creative assets optimized for attention and conversion.

The foundation of AI-driven design is **visual data analysis**. Every color, shape, and composition in an ad affects how audiences perceive it. AI systems trained on billions of images and videos can now detect patterns that humans can't easily quantify. For example, machine-learning models analyze which color palettes increase engagement, what type of imagery drives emotional response, and how composition influences click-through rates. Tools like **EyeQuant**, **Neurons Inc.**, and **Adobe Sensei** use neural networks to simulate human perception—predicting where viewers' eyes will go and how long they'll stay focused. This insight turns visual design from subjective art into measurable science.

AI also plays a vital role in **creative generation**. With tools like **Midjourney**, **Runway**, **Leonardo.ai**, and **Canva Magic Studio**, marketers can produce ad creatives, thumbnails, and video scenes automatically. Instead of spending days on design revisions, you can describe what you need—"a clean, futuristic image of a person using AI technology"—and the AI instantly creates multiple versions in high quality. These tools also allow **style consistency**, ensuring every creative aligns with your brand's color scheme, typography, and visual tone. For campaigns that require large creative volumes—like multi-platform ads—AI generation reduces production time by up to 90%.

Equally transformative is **AI-powered A/B visual testing**. In traditional testing, marketers manually compare two or three images and track performance over time. AI testing expands this exponentially. Systems can test dozens of variations at once, monitoring user engagement metrics such as scroll stop time, hover rate, click-through rate, and conversion lift. As the data comes in, the AI identifies visual trends—like which type of background performs best or which facial expression increases response. It then automatically prioritizes or even regenerates visuals based on what's working. This feedback loop ensures your campaigns stay visually optimized at all times.

Another breakthrough is **predictive visual scoring**. Before an ad even launches, AI can evaluate its design and predict how well it will perform. Using computer vision models trained on thousands of past campaigns, the AI scores each visual asset for emotional impact, clarity, and conversion potential. Designers can then refine weak elements—contrast, focal points, or composition—before spending a dollar on distribution. This preemptive optimization dramatically reduces creative waste and increases the likelihood of success right from launch.

AI also enhances **personalized visual targeting**, adapting designs to different audience segments automatically. A younger demographic might see brighter, high-energy imagery, while a professional audience sees cleaner, minimalistic compositions. Similarly, geographic personalization allows cultural or seasonal design adjustments—snowy winter backdrops for northern regions, tropical tones for southern ones—all managed by AI at scale. This ability to tailor visuals dynamically ensures that every user feels seen and understood.

Finally, visual AI integrates deeply with **creative analytics dashboards**, combining performance data with design insights. These dashboards show which design elements contributed most to conversions, creating an evolving visual intelligence model for your brand. Over time, your system learns exactly what "looks like success"—a unique visual fingerprint that can be replicated across campaigns. This is the point where human creativity and machine intelligence fully converge: you no longer design by guesswork; you design with predictive accuracy.

In essence, AI transforms creative design from reactive to proactive. It doesn't just measure what happened—it predicts what will. For designers and marketers alike, this means freedom. Freedom from endless iterations, subjective debates, and costly delays. The future belongs to brands that combine imagination with data-driven precision, crafting visuals that don't just look beautiful—but perform beautifully, too.

Max Mixes With Midjourney

Max was a talented designer who had built his small studio around passion, not process. His team spent hours perfecting every pixel of ad campaigns for clients, yet results often felt inconsistent. Some ads went viral, others barely performed, and no one could explain why. "Maybe it's luck," his assistant once joked. But deep down, Max knew success wasn't random—it was hidden in patterns they couldn't yet see.

Everything changed the day a client introduced him to AI visual analytics. The client's marketing manager showed him a heatmap generated by a tool called **Neurons Inc.** It displayed exactly where viewers looked on an ad, how long they focused, and which areas they ignored. Max was fascinated. The red zones of attention weren't always where he'd expected. Beautiful designs didn't always perform; simple layouts often did. That realization shook him—and inspired him. He decided to integrate AI into every step of his creative process.

He started by connecting his workflow to **Canva Magic Studio** and **Midjourney**. Now, instead of spending hours brainstorming visuals from scratch, he could describe his ideas and receive dozens of AI-generated concepts within minutes. For one campaign, he typed: "A warm, family-oriented living room with modern eco-friendly furniture and natural sunlight." The results were stunning—each image perfectly balanced lighting, composition, and emotion. What once took his team days now took under an hour.

But the true transformation came with testing. Using an AI-driven visual testing platform, Max uploaded ten design variations for a furniture brand campaign. The system analyzed viewer engagement on each: which colors drew attention, which faces captured emotion, and which layouts drove more clicks. Within hours, it identified a clear winner—an image featuring a smiling couple in a cozy home, surrounded by subtle green tones. The AI even explained why: the composition evoked comfort and aspiration, emotions proven to increase purchase intent. Max felt like he was finally seeing design through his audience's eyes.

Over the next few weeks, he expanded his experiments. For a fashion client, the AI predicted that minimalist flat-lay images would outperform model shots for online ads. The data seemed counterintuitive, but he trusted the process. When the campaign launched, results exceeded expectations—engagement doubled, and sales spiked. The client called it "magic," but Max knew it was method. AI had replaced guesswork with certainty.

He began building a **visual intelligence library** for his agency, storing every creative asset, performance metric, and AI report. Over time, patterns emerged: what colors worked for each industry, what emotional tones resonated with different demographics, what image structures drove conversions. His design decisions became faster, smarter, and undeniably effective. The line between art and analytics blurred—and that was exactly how he liked it.

One day, while presenting results to a major client, Max showed them two ads side by side: one created purely by his team's instinct, the other refined through AI optimization. The AI version had 42% higher engagement. The client was astonished. "How did you know this would perform better?" they asked. Max smiled and replied, "We didn't guess. We learned."

His studio soon became known for combining artistic vision with machine precision. Clients called his approach "creative science." Projects flowed in from around the world, and Max found himself not just designing ads—but designing predictable success. His team no longer argued over subjective choices; they collaborated with data. Every campaign felt like a collaboration between human imagination and artificial intelligence, each sharpening the other.

Months later, as Max watched his latest campaign hit record-breaking results, he reflected on how far he'd come. "AI didn't take my creativity," he thought, "it enhanced it." What used to feel like uncertainty now felt like empowerment. His art had gained a new dimension—not just in beauty, but in impact. For Max, AI wasn't the end of creativity. It was the beginning of intelligent artistry—a world where design didn't just look good; it worked beautifully, every time.

Chapter 10: AI Analytics and Continuous Optimization Systems

In the age of automation, analytics is no longer just a reporting function—it's the living intelligence that drives your entire marketing ecosystem. Data is the DNA of digital advertising, and artificial intelligence has become its central nervous system. While traditional analytics tell you *what* happened, AI analytics explains *why* it happened—and predicts *what will happen next.* This transformation allows marketers to make decisions not based on assumptions, but on evidence and foresight. Continuous optimization, powered by AI, ensures that every campaign, every ad, and every click gets smarter over time.

The foundation of AI analytics lies in **real-time data aggregation and interpretation.** Every digital touchpoint—from ad impressions and video views to page visits and purchases—feeds raw data into your AI system. Unlike manual analytics tools that process daily or weekly summaries, AI systems analyze streams of data live, identifying trends and anomalies as they emerge. This enables marketers to act instantly instead of waiting for end-of-month reports. Platforms like **Google Analytics 4**, **HubSpot AI**, **Sprinklr Insights**, and **Pecan AI** now combine data ingestion with predictive modeling, providing not only visibility but guidance.

One of the greatest strengths of AI analytics is its ability to **connect multi-channel data** into one cohesive view. In the past, marketers had to manually cross-reference numbers from different dashboards—Facebook Ads, Google Ads, TikTok, YouTube, and CRM software—making it almost impossible to see the full customer journey. AI eliminates this fragmentation. By merging all metrics into a single unified model, it can track users across devices and platforms, showing how one ad view on YouTube led to a click on Instagram and a final purchase on desktop. This cross-platform attribution model transforms how marketers understand value and ROI.

The next key component is **predictive analytics.** Using machine learning, AI systems forecast outcomes based on historical patterns. They predict which audiences will convert, which ad creatives will fatigue, and when engagement will peak or drop. Some systems even use **reinforcement learning**, where algorithms test micro-adjustments—such as ad placements, bidding strategies, or creative timing—and continuously learn which combinations yield the best results. This creates a self-optimizing marketing engine that never stops improving, even while you sleep.

Beyond prediction, AI analytics also enables **prescriptive insights**—automated recommendations for what to do next. Instead of simply reporting that "engagement dropped 12%," the system suggests actionable solutions: "Reduce video length to under 15 seconds," or "Reallocate 20% of your budget to high-performing lookalike audiences." This actionable intelligence bridges the gap between analytics and execution, turning data from passive observation into active performance enhancement.

Equally important is **sentiment and behavioral analytics.** AI tools like **Brandwatch**, **Talkwalker**, and **Sprinklr Sentiment AI** analyze public comments, reviews, and social media posts to gauge emotional responses to your brand and campaigns. These models detect tone, mood, and intent—whether customers feel excited, skeptical, or confused—and correlate that sentiment with sales data. For example, if negative feedback spikes after a new ad launch, the system alerts you instantly, allowing quick message adjustments before reputational damage spreads. This emotional intelligence component ensures your marketing remains aligned with audience perception.

Finally, the concept of **continuous optimization systems** brings everything together. Unlike old campaign cycles that ended after launch, AI keeps running perpetual micro-experiments in the background. It constantly tests ad variations, budget shifts, and audience refinements, updating itself with each result. The system becomes a digital marketer that never stops learning—an always-on optimization engine that increases efficiency over time. Over months, this compounding intelligence leads to exponential improvement in ROI, engagement, and overall performance.

In short, AI analytics turns marketing from reactive to proactive. It empowers decision-makers not just to measure results but to engineer them. Through automation, prediction, and continuous learning, AI doesn't replace the marketer—it elevates them to strategist, innovator, and architect of systems that think, adapt, and win continuously. In this new paradigm, success is not achieved once—it is maintained indefinitely through intelligent evolution.

How to Fix Them

David had been in marketing for over fifteen years. He'd seen trends come and go—SEO booms, social media explosions, influencer waves—but one thing remained constant: the struggle to understand data. Every week, he stared at spreadsheets from different ad platforms, trying to piece together what was really driving his results. It felt like detective work with missing clues. "We have all the numbers," he often said, "but none of the answers." That changed the day his agency adopted an AI analytics system. At first, David was skeptical. He had used automation tools before, but they always felt like glorified dashboards. This was different. The system didn't just show graphs–it explained them. Within hours of integration, it had analyzed months of data across Meta, Google, TikTok, and YouTube, then produced a single report titled: *'Why Your Campaigns Are Underperforming–and How to Fix Them.'* It identified patterns David had never noticed: engagement on weekends was strong, but conversions dipped because the checkout process slowed on mobile. The AI even suggested optimizing the mobile flow and reallocating budget to weekday retargeting. He followed its advice–and conversions jumped 27% within a week.

Soon, the AI became his silent strategist. Each morning, it delivered a summary: "Yesterday's top performer: TikTok short video. Suggested action: Increase daily spend by 15%." It highlighted trends in real time, predicting when ad fatigue would hit and which creatives were likely to decline next. For the first time, David wasn't reacting–he was anticipating. The stress of uncertainty was replaced by clarity and control.

As the weeks passed, the system began learning his agency's unique rhythm. It understood seasonal cycles, client industries, and even emotional audience patterns. During one campaign for a fitness brand, it alerted David that sentiment around "extreme transformations" was turning negative in comments. It recommended shifting messaging toward "small wins and sustainable progress." He made the change overnight–and engagement surged back. The AI wasn't just reading data; it was reading emotion.

Over time, David's agency transformed from reactive to predictive. Instead of waiting for campaigns to fail before fixing them, his team optimized continuously, guided by AI insights. They built dashboards that visualized everything: which ad formats drove the most conversions, which customer journeys were most profitable, and how each creative decision affected sales. Clients began to notice. During meetings, David could now show projections with 95% accuracy, supported by real-time graphs that updated as he spoke. "It's like the future already knows our numbers," one client joked.

What amazed David most was the compounding effect. Every campaign taught the AI something new, which improved the next one. Six months later, their return on ad spend had doubled while manual workload dropped by half. His team, once buried in data cleanup, now spent their days strategizing and experimenting. "We've gone from data entry to data mastery," David told his staff.

One evening, as he reviewed his dashboard, David reflected on how far marketing had come. Gone were the days of waiting for reports or guessing what might work. The system in front of him was alive—constantly learning, optimizing, and evolving. It didn't just analyze data; it empowered him to think bigger, to focus on creativity, innovation, and long-term vision.

Looking at the graphs rising steadily upward, he smiled and whispered, "This is what control feels like." The AI had given him back what every marketer craves but rarely achieves—predictability. His campaigns no longer lived or died by chance; they grew, adapted, and thrived through continuous intelligence.

For David, AI wasn't just a tool—it was a transformation. It had turned chaos into clarity, guesswork into science, and performance into progress. And as he prepared his next campaign, he realized the truth: in a world where algorithms evolve every second, success belongs to those who evolve with them.

Epilogue

The Future of AI in Social Media Advertising

The age of artificial intelligence has only just begun, yet it has already redefined the very foundation of social media advertising. What was once a world of guesswork and intuition has become an ecosystem of intelligence—data-driven, automated, and infinitely adaptable. Each chapter of this book represents a stepping stone toward a future where creativity and computation merge seamlessly. But as powerful as these technologies have become, their true potential lies not in replacing human marketers, but in amplifying them—turning insight into foresight, and imagination into measurable impact.

The future of AI in social media advertising will be defined by **integration, personalization, and ethical intelligence**. We are entering an era where every brand will operate as a living system—a digital organism that learns, predicts, and adapts to its audience in real time. AI will not just manage campaigns; it will craft experiences. Instead of ads interrupting users' feeds, they will blend into conversations, tailored perfectly to context and mood. Personalized video ads will be generated on the fly for each viewer, using dynamic scripts, visuals, and even AI voiceovers that match their interests, tone, and timing. This is not science fiction; it is already taking shape.

At the heart of this revolution lies **predictive empathy**—AI's ability to anticipate not just what people want, but how they feel. Emotional intelligence algorithms are being trained to detect subtle human signals—facial expressions, sentiment shifts, micro-interactions—and adjust ad messaging accordingly. Imagine an AI system that recognizes when a user is overwhelmed, tired, or optimistic, and responds with content designed to uplift, inspire, or motivate. The best ads of tomorrow won't sell—they will serve. They will meet people where they are emotionally, delivering value first and profit second.

AI's future in advertising also points toward **fully autonomous marketing ecosystems**. These self-optimizing systems will oversee entire brand strategies—from audience research and creative design to testing, budgeting, and analytics—without constant human oversight. Yet, the most successful brands will not surrender creativity to automation; they will use AI as a creative collaborator. The future belongs to those who understand how to **direct the intelligence**, not just deploy it. Marketers will become orchestrators of digital ecosystems, curating ideas, fine-tuning emotions, and shaping human-AI partnerships into something beautiful and effective.

Another emerging frontier is **AI-generated storytelling**. With advancements in multimodal models—systems capable of producing synchronized text, visuals, voice, and video—brands will be able to create entire ad campaigns from a single concept input. A marketer will describe the goal ("Create a 15-second TikTok about confidence using my brand colors and slogan"), and AI will generate multiple professional-quality versions instantly. Each will then be automatically tested, refined, and scaled, guided by live engagement data. What once required agencies, focus groups, and weeks of work will soon happen in minutes.

Ethics will play an equally crucial role in this new world. As AI gains access to personal behavior data, transparency and consent will become non-negotiable. The future of advertising must balance intelligence with integrity. The brands that thrive will be those that treat data as a privilege, not a possession—those that use AI to help customers make better choices rather than manipulate them into more purchases. In an age of algorithmic power, **trust will be the new currency**. Customers will stay loyal not to the flashiest brands, but to the most authentic and transparent ones.

We are also witnessing the rise of **AI democratization**—a world where advanced tools once reserved for corporations become available to everyone. Small businesses, freelancers, and creators will soon have access to enterprise-level AI systems capable of designing, testing, and scaling global campaigns. This means the next big brand might not come from a Fortune 500 company, but from a single individual with an idea, a laptop, and an AI toolkit. The playing field is leveling, and creativity—not capital—will determine success.

Looking ahead, **the convergence of AI, augmented reality (AR), and the metaverse** will open entirely new dimensions for engagement. Consumers will no longer just watch ads; they will experience them. Virtual stores, interactive campaigns, and personalized 3D environments will allow users to "step inside" a brand story. AI will power these immersive experiences, learning from every movement, glance, and gesture to tailor what the user sees next. The future of social media advertising will not live on screens—it will live all around us.

Yet, amid this wave of automation and advancement, one truth will always remain: **creativity is human**. AI can generate infinite variations, but it is our stories, emotions, and authenticity that give meaning to those creations. The marketer of tomorrow will not be a coder or technician but a visionary—a storyteller armed with tools of limitless scale and precision. The more AI evolves, the more human creativity will matter. Because technology may amplify the voice, but it is humanity that gives it something worth saying.

As we step into this next chapter of marketing history, the question is no longer whether AI will dominate advertising—it already has. The real question is: *how will you use it?* Will you resist it, letting automation outpace your adaptability? Or will you embrace it—learning, experimenting, and collaborating with it to create campaigns that resonate across generations? The future belongs to the latter. The marketers who master AI will not just stay relevant—they will lead, inspire, and redefine what connection means in a digital world.

The evolution of advertising is no longer about technology—it's about transformation. It's about using intelligence not to shout louder but to listen better, not to manipulate but to understand. The tools have changed, but the goal remains the same: to connect people through stories that matter. The next frontier of social media advertising is already here. It is intelligent, automated, and deeply human—and you are now ready to shape it.

www.ingramcontent.com/pod-product-compliance
Lightning Source LLC
LaVergne TN
LVHW022018200926
848481LV00007B/2446
* 9 7 9 8 2 9 5 4 2 3 3 0 7 *